Life-Changing Classics, Volume XI

The Price
OF LEADERSHIP

Charlie "Tremendous" Jones

TREMENDOUS
LIFE BOOKS.com

Life-Changing Classics, Volume XI
The Price of Leadership

Published by
Tremendous Life Books
206 West Allen Street
Mechanicsburg, PA 17055
717-766-9499   800-233-2665
Fax: 717-766-6565
www.TremendousLifeBooks.com

ISBN: 978-1-936354-01-6

Printed in the United States of America

Table of Contents

Foreword

I heard my father deliver the "Price of Leadership" speech hundreds of times. As a child, I remember listening in wonderment at the price required to be a leader. During my teens, the wonderment turned to apprehension as I began to comprehend more and more of the message. I thought leadership was supposed to be all about power and prestige, so I didn't understand why the price was so daunting.

It wasn't until my professional years that I began to glimpse the price you must pay in order to be a leader. Growing up, my father showed me through his life that it required loneliness, weariness, abandonment, and vision. It's only when you are *willing and begin* to take the action required that you understand the price of leadership.

This speech originated when my father was fresh from the trenches of the life insurance industry. He loved this industry, and it produced some of the greatest salespeople ever. His stories reflect the activities and responses of a young salesman passionate about sharing with others the security he found in the industry. It also includes a very pragmatic and humorous assessment of things that come out of employees' and prospects' mouths and how to stay motivated regardless.

The greatest takeaway from this little speech is that the next time you sit in your office alone, with your forehead in your hands, abandoned by the very ones you're trying so hard to assist, so tired you don't think you can go on—and you're the only one who seems to grasp the vision of what needs to be done—know that you are truly on the road to learning what it takes to pay the price of leadership. And know that you are learning to really live!

Tracey Jones
President, Tremendous Life Books

Biography of
Charlie "Tremendous" Jones

Charlie "Tremendous" Jones entered the gates of Heaven on October 16, 2008. He made his mark as a best-selling author, publisher, and internationally acclaimed motivational speaker who gained a reputation as an inspirational humorist and book evangelist.

Charles E. Jones was born in Alabama and grew up in Pennsylvania. His beloved wife Gloria resides in Mechanicsburg, Pennsylvania. Their marriage produced six children and six grandchildren.

Before achieving tremendous success as a motivational speaker, Charlie Jones started off as an insurance salesman. In 1950—just one year after entering the insurance business with one of America's top-ten companies—he was awarded his agency's Most Valuable Associate award at the age of 23. Ten years later Mr. Jones received his company's highest management award for recruiting, manpower and development, and business management.

At age 37 his organization exceeded $100 million in force, at which time he founded Life

The Price of Leadership

Management Services to share his experiences through seminars and consulting.

For more than a quarter of a century, thousands of audiences in America, Canada, Mexico, Australia, New Zealand, Europe, and Asia experienced nonstop laughter as Mr. Tremendous shared his ideas about life's most challenging situations in business and at home.

He is the author of *Life Is Tremendous*, a best-selling book about his 7 Laws of Leadership, with more than 3 million copies in print. Two of his speeches, "The Price of Leadership" and "Where Does Leadership Begin?" have been enjoyed by millions on audio recordings and at conventions.

He was featured on a variety of radio programs, television networks, and films ranging from the *Dynamic Achievers World Network* television series to the *Insights into Excellence* video training series.

The University of Southern California, University of Tennessee, and Pensacola Christian College are just a few of the institutions where Mr. Jones was featured as a guest lecturer.

He also served on the advisory boards of several organizations and was the president and founder of Life Management Services Inc. as well as Executive Books (now Tremendous Life Books) in Mechanicsburg, Pennsylvania.

Charlie "Tremendous" Jones

In addition to being a dynamic speaker and businessman, Mr. Jones was also a great humanitarian, with a passion for helping individuals understand the value of reading. It was Mac McMillon whom Mr. Jones first heard say, "You are today what you'll be five years from now, except for the people you meet and the books you read." This statement eventually became one of Mr. Jones's most quoted lines as he inspired individuals all over the world to read.

Through his publishing company and bookstore, Executive Books, Mr. Jones gave away millions of books, fulfilling his mission as a book evangelist. In addition to the generous donations the company still makes, the book business that Mr. Tremendous originated is presently thriving and generating millions of dollars in annual revenues under the direction of his daughter, Tracey Jones.

For more than 50 years Charlie "Tremendous" Jones was passionate about exciting people to read, think, and share. In 2002 he received a Doctor of Humane Letters degree from Central Pennsylvania College, and in 2003 the college's new library was named the Charles "T" Jones Leadership Library in recognition of his love for reading and sharing great books.

The Price of Leadership

"A good character is the best tombstone.
Those who loved you and were helped
by you will remember you when forget-
me-nots have withered. Carve your
name on hearts, not on marble."
—Charles Spurgeon

I'd like to talk about the word "leadership," but not because I'm an authority on it. Sometimes someone will say to me, "Jones, I understand you're going to speak on leadership? Aren't you rather young to speak as an authority on the word 'leadership'?" Yes, I am. But I'm not speaking as an authority; I'm speaking as a student.

I speak on the subject of leadership because I believe it's a tremendously important and misunderstood word. I approach it as a student, like the young minister preparing for his first sermon. He was in seminary preparing for that great day when he would stand before the congregation and lower the boom, telling them how to start living. He polished the sermon. He refined it. It was really getting better, week after week, month after month, and then the great day came. After two or three minutes, he realized he was in deep trouble. He began to feel around on the podium for a button he could push that would open the trap door and let him slip out of sight. But there wasn't any push button. Within five minutes he realized he was whipped and that things were different in real life than they were in seminary. He said a hasty benediction and went down off the platform beaten, broken, and dejected. As he departed the podium, one of the old gray-headed warhorses slipped his arm over the young minister's shoulder and whispered in his ear, "Son, if you'd have gone up like you came down, you could have come down like you went up."

Now that's a good attitude to approach any subject with, isn't it? Humility, servitude—the realization that there is a great deal you don't know even as a leader, a teacher, a pastor, or a parent. Well, that's the attitude I approach the subject of leadership with. *Leadership*. That's a big word, and a lot has been written on it. The reason that I particularly like to speak on the subject is that I find, in my experience, leadership is the most misunderstood and misrepresented word in our

vocabulary. My experiences especially bea.
out, and I'll tell you why.

When I was growing up my dad used to say
something like, "Son, it's about time you started
acting like a man." I thought, *That's a good idea,
Dad. What's a man supposed to act like?* And so I
began to look around to observe what men acted
like. As I looked around, I learned to act like men
were acting and I soon became one of the actors.
Then some years later I discovered that one of
life's greatest challenges, if not life's *greatest*
challenge, was how to quit acting and start being.
Isn't that something? I heard that you are the sum
total of all you think about. I heard people say,
"There's a fellow who has it. He's a natural if
I ever saw one!" I thought, *Whatever he has is
what I've got to get because that's what I want!*
So I began to look and search and to really live,
and I began to learn about the various leadership
cults.

The first cult of leadership I discovered was
the personality cult. This one is attractive because
you've got to dress the part. You've got to walk
the part. You've got to talk the part. You've got
to think the part. People will say, "Whoo-wee,
he has it!" This is the group that's standing in
front of the mirror every day chanting, "Come
on, beauty boy, you can do it!" Then they flop

because they never get out of the house. That would be funny except all across the country there are people who are learning to look exactly what a leader ought to look like on the outside, but they never begin to learn the person a leader ought to be. Isn't that sad?

I got out of that cult. That cost me a lot of money. Do you know what the next cult was? The title cult. Sometimes you go to a meeting and a guy says, "You want to know why I'm not successful?" Why? "Because, I don't have any title." I thought, *Well maybe that's what I need: a title.* For seven years I burned up the roads in our county. I mean to tell you I was everywhere all the time. Finally, the vice president saw the light. They called me in. They said, "Come in here, Jones." Yes sir. "Jones, how would you like to be our leader down in Harrisburg?" I jumped in my car. I sped down the New Jersey Turnpike, I was sure to have a heart attack before I got there. Their leader was on the way! Off to Harrisburg, up the elevator, into the manager's office. Your leader has arrived! But not a lousy soul would follow me! All that for nothing! That would be even funnier except that sort of tragedy happens all across America, in government, in church, in business. You find people burning out the lights to get a title, only to get it and not know what to do with it when they got it.

Well, I got out of that cult. That cost me another fortune. I found another cult, the endowment cult. This one states, "Some have it, some don't." I already knew I didn't have it.

I can't tell you all that leadership is, but I can tell you what it isn't. Leadership isn't personality. Leadership isn't title. Leadership isn't endowment. Leadership is that something bought with a price that can be paid for by anybody, anytime, anyplace. A man is as much of a leader today as he is ever going to be because the price he is paying right now is determining the kind of leader he is going to be tomorrow. Isn't that something? And listen to this: Every man has an obligation, as well as a privilege, to be a leader in something. Everybody, you ask? Yes, everybody.

You may wonder what you can be a leader in. Well, you can at least be a leader in failures! Why would anyone want to be a leader in failure? If you're a leader in failures long enough you'll get recognized.

You ask, "Is there anything else I can lead in?" Yes, you can do as I did when I was a twenty-two-year-old kid wondering what I could lead in. I looked around and noticed there were so many things that nobody was doing. I knew that anyone can lead in something if they want to, can't they?

The Price of Leadership

I just found something that nobody else was doing, I did it, and that made me the leader. You say, what does that prove? It proved at least to my eyes that I wanted to be better. Look at the number of people who go through life never really knowing what it is to have a burning desire to be better.

What is leadership? Leadership is something that belongs to the fellow who paves the way, who sets the pace, who goes ahead. He doesn't need any title to do that. He doesn't need any endowment. He doesn't need any personality. You always find, in every agency, there's a group of fellows who are willing to go ahead. Notice I said "willing," not able. You already know there are always a lot of people who are able, but they're not willing. It would be wonderful if you had a lot of able *and* willing people, but too many times, it falls on those who are willing. The fellow who is willing to go ahead and set the pace is the leader, whether he likes it or not. Because it's not a title, it's not a personality, it's not an endowment. It's just the price he paid to *go ahead*.

What *is* this price of leadership that is so terrible we lose ourselves in many blind alleys, leading us nowhere? I'm sure there are many things that could be added to my list, but experience has taught me that the price of leadership is—

Charlie "Tremendous" Jones

Loneliness
Weariness
Abandonment
Vision

The price of leadership begins with *loneliness*. LONELINESS. What is leadership? What does a leader do? A leader is simply one who goes ahead, one who sets the pace, paves the way, and influences others to follow. Once we decide to set the pace and move ahead, we discover why most refuse to pay the first price of leadership: Being a leader can be a very *lonely* job at times—so lonely that many return to the pack only to discover too late that the pack isn't going anywhere. They want to make sure of the end before going off into the terrible unknown where it is *lonely*. Another phrase we often hear is "I won't go ahead until I know I'm right." Seems strange how slowly we realize how many times the very things that appeared so wrong turned out so right, and the things that appeared so right turned out so wrong. We definitely need to avoid unnecessary trial and error as much as possible, but we cannot let the fear of failure cripple us. I've come to the conclusion that in some cases we won't know for sure until the end what is the right method or the wrong method, and the end might be a long way off.

The Price of Leadership

Loneliness is the first price of leadership. A fellow said, "Did you say 'loneliness'?" Yes, I did. You say, "I'm glad you said that! If loneliness is the first price of leadership, I must be a dynamic leader because I am really lonely!" I don't mean that kind of loneliness. Everybody is lonely like that. I used to think I was the only one who was lonely. Then you figure out that everybody is lonely. You know what the old-timers tell me? Not only is life lonely, it's going to get lonelier! How about that? I can hardly stand how lonely I am now. My loneliness came from my inferiority complex. Did you hear about the fellow who went in to see the psychiatrist about his inferiority complex? He walks out of the doctor's office exclaiming, "I'm so happy, I'm so happy!" A passerby asks, "Why?" The man says, "I just went to see my psychiatrist about my inferiority complex and he told me I don't have a complex. I'm just inferior!"

I used to look at all the superior people; I mean all the people who acted superior. But you see, so many have learned to act so superior, and I knew I was so inferior. I realized I had to learn to act as superior as you so you would never find out how inferior I was. Then I wouldn't be lonely. Soon I learned to act better than most of you. I looked around and noticed that you were inferior and I was superior. All that for nothing! Isn't that something? No wonder life is so lonely. You see, the problem is that we grow up. Once upon a time we were little boys and little girls and we grew up; physically, that is, not emotionally. And we have this little barrier that we build and we never let anybody really know who we truly are. Isn't it amazing how men and women can live together and have children together and never know each other? We never really let anybody in that little barrier. We always have that barrier up, and the desire in my heart is, "Won't somebody get to know me? Please, get to know me." Then what happens when you decide to get to know me? When you start getting to know me, I don't really want you to really get to know me. Because if you really get to know me, you won't like me! So I'm mad at you if you don't try to get to know me, I'm mad at you if you do try to get to know me, I'm mad at you no matter what you do. I guess that's why a lot of people go through life just mad.

Now, I don't want to major in loneliness. I just want to make the point that everybody is lonely. That's why half of the hospital beds in America are filled with people who are dying of something when there's nothing visibly wrong with them—dying from the wrong disease, from the wrong type of loneliness. And yet for everyone in every church, in every community, and every agency, there are a million things for folks to be doing. And what do we do? Sit around in our own little world, sucking our thumbs, going through our paralytic, anemic act, dying for the wrong purpose. Leadership, you see, begins with loneliness, too.

We're all going to know an inevitable loneliness, but I'm talking about a loneliness you choose. The loneliness that comes to the fellow who says, "I'm going to do this. I'm going to make my mark. I'm going to set the pace. This is where I'm going to make my stand. This is what I'm going to contribute." There is no one who can lead in your church or your agency the way you can. There's no one who can lead in the things that you lead in. No one can get your rewards if you're not leading in the things that you and you alone can do. What you are a part of will never be what it was meant to be if you are on the fence about leading.

What's the first thing a fellow learns when he says, "Okay, I'm going to bring this home. I'm really going to take the bait. I'm going to set the pace"? He discovers it's lonely and he doesn't like being lonely. So what does he do? He rushes back and says, "I'm going to go back and lead with a committee!" You can't lead with a committee. Why? The committee isn't going anywhere. Has the committee ever gone anywhere? No. Will a committee ever go anywhere? No. Why? God never promised to bless a committee or a group. God promised to bless the hearts of men. Now, a great committee or a great agency or a great community is a group of individuals who want their lives to count for something individually. We all know what it is to pay the price of loneliness. As we move forward, it requires that we make a decision to take action.

The guy says, "Charlie, boy, did you hit the nail on the head there. That's my big problem." "What's that?" I ask. "Getting started!" I know just what you're talking about. I'm an authority on that. I'm going to write a book titled *10,000 New Reasons How Not to Get Started*. You say, "Why don't you write a book on how to get started?" I can't because no one knows how to get started! Nobody ever really got started. Did you know that? You know why most men fail in life? Most men fail not because they failed; most men fail simply because they never got started. How long does a man have to live before he learns if a fellow ever gets started, he's about home already! How long does a man have to live before he learns that 95 percent of all the energy he will ever expend on a project will be expended on getting started? It's the same principle as flying to L.A. or home to Baltimore. It's all about the power to take off, to get airborne, and then you coast while making course corrections. That's the way of getting it done.

A young guy came up to me one time and said, "Charlie, how long did it take you to get started?" I said, "I'll be honest with you. I never got started yet, but when I do, watch my smoke!" You say, "Wait a minute! If you never got started, how did you get so successful?" Well, I watched all these guys try to get started and they couldn't get started. So they up and quit. What I chose to do when I couldn't get started after five or six years was that I just learned how to *get started getting started*, and nobody ever knew the difference!

You'll never reach a plateau when you can say, "I'm on my way forever. I never have to suit up anymore." One of the greatest things in life to learn is that life isn't for riding. Life is for being on the way, and the fellow who is learning how to *get started getting started* has accessed one of the great crossroads of his life. That's right. Another fellow once said to me, "You know what my problem is?" What's your problem? "Well, my problem is I'm sort of a perfectionist. I believe when I make a decision, it's got to be the right decision. I do things right the first time." Don't those guys kill you? Always trying to figure out how to make a right decision. In building my agency during my sales years, I never did figure out how to make a right decision.

All of the things I thought were going to turn out right, turned out wrong. Most of the things I thought were going to turn out wrong, turned out right. Then I thought I wouldn't know what's going to turn out right or wrong until the end, and the end ain't here yet. I think you would agree that of all the people you and I have met across the country in our travels, we have never met a man that God put a head on his shoulders who was brilliant enough to know how to make a right decision. But you know what I found? I found that even though God never made the man who knew how to make a right decision, he made a lot of men who know how to make decisions and make them right.

An awful lot of time is wasted worrying about how to make the right decision that will never be made. But a man can learn how to get started getting started, make a decision, and then go on making it right. I guess that's pretty simple, isn't it? When a man makes a decision to get going, to get started, to make his decision, to make it right, he makes a decision.

The Price of Leadership

Paying the price begins with a *decision*. We must decide to *act*—to get on with the show—or our most tremendous dreams and ambitions will profit us nothing. The person willing to pay the price must realize that loneliness is a plague that is known to all, but *leaders* choose a different type of loneliness that separates them into a small corps. Decision making is another subject, but for our purpose I think we should think about the three facets of decision making.

There's three parts to decision making. The first part is to make it; the second part is to make it yours. This is the age of "let's sleep on it," "let's talk it over." You may ask, "Don't you believe in talking things over?" Yes I do. I believe in talking things over with people who have done what I want to do. I believe in talking things over with people who have paid the price I want to pay. But I do not believe in talking things over with anybody who hasn't done what I want to do or hasn't paid the price I want to pay. What do I have to talk over with them? I find that most men are talking things over with people who are going to talk him out of it, rather than into it.

Here's a good illustration of this. Why did so many men leave the life insurance business last year? Another thing I heard last year was that there are fewer men selling life insurance today than there were ten years ago. I can't believe that. I cannot believe that except I know that's true, and I think I know why it's true. I believe companies are wasting their money if they are depending on management to sell people on coming into the life insurance business. Do you know why I say that? I believe the greatest recruiters in the world are not staff people, or managers, or general agents. I believe the greatest recruiters in the world are the people doing the job. My first year in the life insurance selling field, I recruited more full-time men for my agency than two full-time salaried recruiters. The guy says why did you do that? Well, you know, misery loves company! I'll tell you why I did it. I believe a man is a fraud who would take a commission for selling something and not want to share his career with somebody who will never know our joys unless we share it with them.

Later I went into management. I loved to share the business. A fellow comes up to me and says, "Wait a minute, Jones. If you like to sell so much, how come you left the field?" I said, "I ran out of friends and relatives!"

When I went into management I'd have a fellow sitting in my office. I'd tell him about the freedom, the dole, the prestige, and laughing all the way to the bank on Friday. His eyes would begin to light up. His smile would begin to come across his face and I would say, "What do you think?" "It sounds tremendous to me." "Okay, sign your name right here." He'd say, "Wait!" I'd say, "What do you mean, 'Wait'?" "I want to talk it over with my wife!" Your wife? You know why God didn't make your wife a man? You don't need another husband! You know why American women have to take over the church and the government and the business? Because Papa won't pop!

Now let me explain what I said. Somebody said I bet he doesn't get along well at home these days. We do. I love Gloria more today than I ever loved her. Twenty years have gone by. She is the doll of dolls. She is the sweetest thing. We don't need a second honeymoon, we're on it! She is tremendous! We have six children. We have them in college and down in the crib, five months old. I tell you she's the greatest housekeeper. She's the greatest homemaker. She's the greatest baby maker, you name it! She is fantabulously tremendous. She is really something.

Now, let me show you what I mean. Suppose tomorrow morning I'm in the office and the phone rings and I say, "Hello?" And a voice on the other end says, "Honey, honey, oh!!" I say, "What's wrong?" "Oh, oh honey, honey, honey.

Charlie "Tremendous" Jones

Our little baby Tracey has a rear-end rash!" Now what do I know about rear-end rashes? My wife is an authority on rear-end rashes. She doesn't need to consult me about rear-end rashes. My wife has the authority to make all rear-end-rash decisions! Now, there *are* a few areas I'm an authority in.

Do you know a lot of people don't realize that we all have problems? Did you know everybody has problems? I hope you do. If you think you're the only one, you're mistaken. I want to tell you that not only do you have problems, I have news for you: they are going to get worse! You say, "Wait a minute, wait a minute. I thought you were supposed to refresh us and encourage us!" I'm not here to refresh and encourage you. I'm here to salve your wounds and get you ready for the next onslaught.

Now, when I have a problem, am I supposed to go to my dear little wife with the kind of problem that weighs you down, that breaks your back, and pushes you to the agonizing depths of despair? Am I supposed to go, "Honey, honey, I can't go on much longer! You're going to help me with these decisions!" Wait a minute! When I get to be sixty-five, I may be the biggest flop the world has ever known, but I'm going to get all the credit! Can't you just see a guy at sixty-five, rocking back and forth with his little sweetie pie, and he looks over at her and says, "You know, honey, I would have been a dynamic success except for your lousy decisions."

Now burn this into your heart. When you make a decision, make it yours. Do you know why? You'll only die for your decisions. Does this mean you're an isolationist or a nonconformist? No. But it means that there are some things you and you alone are responsible for and you cannot shoulder it to somebody else.

Do you know why a lot of people are leaving the things that they started to do? Because they realize after they got started that somebody talked them into it. Don't you ever let anybody talk you into anything! You make your decision and make it yours. Did you know that behind every successful man stands a surprised mother-in-law!

Make your decisions and make them yours. And remember, sometimes you will make a right decision in life that will seem wrong for a long time after you made it. Right decisions mean there is going to be some growing to do. When there is growing, you're going through valleys. It's a fact that when no one understands a decision and it looks as though this thing can't work out, they look around for whom to blame. Who talked you into it? But if you talked yourself into it, you'll die before you admit you're wrong.

Charlie "Tremendous" Jones

Think about it. Make it, make your decision and make it yours.

Third, the most important part . . .

Die by it! Stick by it! Burn this one into your heart. Stickability! There's a plague now sweeping the world. It's a terrible plague. I understand that it has reached epidemic proportions in many communities. The plague is known commonly as the quitter's disease. Everywhere I go I hear people saying, "I quit, I quit, I quit, I quit, I quit, I quit!" I expect to go into the office tomorrow and a guy will meet me at the door and say, "Hello, Charlie, I quit!" What, you quit again? What did you quit for this time? The guy said, "Don't you joke about quitting. Don't you realize how serious that is?" I sure do know how serious it is! The guy says, "Didn't you ever want to quit?" Yes! I'm the world's number-one quitter. I've always wanted to quit. Who wouldn't want to quit? If you had to go through what I had to go through my first year, you would have to be crazy not to want to quit.

Once in a while you go to a seminar and some guy gets up and says, "I love challenge!" Don't you hate those birdbrains? I hate challenge! I've always hated challenge. You know what I love? I love results! Mmmm. That's what I love. I love results so much, I'll put up with all of the challenge in the world to get a little result. Don't

The Price of Leadership

ou pity the mutton-heads who love challenge and no results? Deliver me from them! But in the beginning of my career it was almost always challenge and no results. Who wouldn't want to quit? I used to want to quit in the morning; I used to want to quit in the afternoon; I'd want to quit at night. I always wanted to quit. Who wouldn't want to quit? I used to be driving down the road thinking there's a reason I ought to quit. There's another reason I ought to quit. There's one I never even thought of before! I don't know how I've gone on this long! You know what used to get me? The more I'd wanted to quit, the more I would want to quit; and the more I would want to quit, the more I was afraid I was going to quit; and I didn't want to quit, I just wanted to want to quit! And one day I learned that there's a difference between quitting and wanting to quit. What did I do? I decided I'll never, never, never, never quit, and since then I've been able to enjoy wanting to quit because I know I'm not going to quit! That's made me a fortune.

Make a decision. Make it yours and die by it. You know there are only three decisions in life. You say, "Wait a minute, wait a minute, I made thirty yesterday." There are only three decisions, and when a man makes the three basic decisions in life, he no longer has any more choices. His life becomes one of necessity—one of compulsion, compelling, and constraining.

What are those three decisions?

Who are you going to live your life with?

What are you going to live your life in?

And *what are you going to live your life for?*

You know, it's just amazing. I was in Seattle this morning. The magazines aren't too bad this month because they change them, but normally I never read the articles. The titles are enough to kill you. In every one of these magazines there's always one article about what is the secret to a successful marriage. Guess what it is? Compatibility.

Compatibility. That is the biggest lie I've ever heard! Why, if compatibility is a secret to a successful marriage, I would be the most miserable man in town.

I want to tell you this thought. Before my wife and I were married, we were compatible. We were so compatible it hurt. Before we were married, she loved to have my way. What was the first thing I found out when we got married? She had a way and she liked it. I can show you the spot where my wife sat and looked up into my eyes and said, "My dearest, I understand you so well." How about that? I don't even understand myself. I married her on that alone. And what was the first thing that I learned after we got married? She lied! No sooner did we get married I realized it was all a miserable mistake. Now, according to what people say, you've got to be compatible. If you're not compatible, trade her in, get a new model. I'm not doing that. I have an investment here, brother. I decided to rehabilitate her. But I failed, like you! Then she rehabilitated me, and since then I've been so happy I can't stand it!

You know what went wrong? I'll tell you what went wrong. I knew I was a mouse, but I knew with her help, she would bring out these masculine qualities in me and I could be the man that she thought I was before she found out she married a mouse. Is it my fault she found out the truth too soon? I didn't get what I thought I was getting either. She fooled me and I fooled her, and there we were—stuck. We deserved each other. Now here's what went wrong. I knew I needed her to make me better. I married her to help make me better. And she married me. She knew that she needed me to help make her better. But that's where she fouled it up. Because she wouldn't let me change her and make her better until I let her change me and make me better! Nothing doing . . . I'm dying this way!

And that's why you hardly ever find a happy home. Very few people know that marriage is not a honeymoon, it's warfare! Life isn't compatibility. A guy says, "I wish I could get somebody who will accept me for me." You'd better hope you never get anybody that low! When two people come together, they come to grow together. Growing means growing pains. And if they don't allow each other to change each other, they wind up fighting to change each other. Listen. The key to a successful marriage is not compatibility. It's commitment. Make a decision and make it yours and die by it. When my wife married me, it was for better, for worse, mostly worse; richer or poorer, mostly poorer; 'til death do us part, that settles that.

Now our patience is being rewarded. With all my heart, I wish young people could know this. I wish somebody would tell them what growing is, what integrity means. That's nonsense about compatibility and why people will never fit each other. This is what brings about growth. I was married seven years before I ever talked to my wife. The guy says, "You must have had a silent marriage." No, it was very noisy. We just never talked to each other. We were married about seven years before we ever learned to really talk with each other. I mean really talk and really get to each other's hearts.

I was lecturing all over America on confidence

and courage, and I never had enough courage to pray with my own family and wife. It took me three years of battling to get up enough courage to pray with them. One night I remember hearing my wife pray something. I was irritated with some little thing, and I heard her say, "Dear God, thank you for this good husband. Forgive me for not being a better wife." And I'll never forget it. I was so crushed it broke my heart. I realized I was a scoundrel, a mutton-head. *I* was the one who wasn't the right kind of husband or father. One of the greatest things in all the world that a man can ever have is someone to grow old with him. I wish people would know that compatibility is not the key; it's coming together, staying together, and growing together. Who are you going to live your life with? Who are you going to get up every day of your life with?

Do you know why I draw this marriage analogy out? I like to take this marriage analogy and make it applicable to a man's business life. Who are you going to live your life with? What are going to do? What are you going to be?

Once in a while you hear a guy say, "I don't think I'm fit for this business." You had better hope you don't get what business you're fit for either. Or you hear a guy say, "Enough of these guys that put their job ahead of their family; not me, brother!" Don't you ever tell me that! You know why a guy better never tell me he puts anything ahead of his job? He better never even tell me he puts his church ahead of his job. Do you know why? I never saw a man who was any good at anything who wasn't good on his job. A man must learn that a job is just a sacred a trust as marriage. He's got to learn to love and honor and cherish his job, just like his marriage. If he doesn't, his job won't reward him anymore than his marriage, unless he does the same thing with it. That's not easy to learn. That's not talked about much. People who live in the realm of reality know it's true.

Show me a man who works, who knows what it's like to put his hand on a plow, and I'll show you a fellow who's learning great lessons for his family and his church. Show me a man who talks about what he puts first ahead of his job, I'll show you a guy who doesn't put anything first but himself.

I get a kick out of all the people looking for the right job. You probably know a lot of people who say, "I don't think I'm in the right job." The right job? There is no such thing as the right job! God never made a right job. God never made a job that would make a man, but he made any man who could make a job. You've got to be faithful to it.

The Price of Leadership

You've got to be committed to it. You've got to love it. "But," you say, "It's not what I thought." Well, that's the idea of making it!

Did you ever figure out why so many fellows are leaving the life insurance business? Here's a perfect example: "Good morning, Mr. Manager. My wife said I'm to come down here. I've been unemployed at the plant. My neighbor drives a Cadillac and he sleeps in late. He's in this insurance racket and says I'm supposed to try this out, and if I like it I'm going to stay on." And the manager thinks, *Hmmm, right in the middle of the recruiting drive, a million-dollar producer walks in. Whew!* Now that's like me saying to my wife, "Honey, I'm lonely. I haven't done anything for two months and I'm just a little lonely. I decided I'm going to try you out, and if I like you I'll keep you." You can't try out a marriage, and you can't try out a job. You give yourself to a job and you give yourself to a marriage. It works that way.

Now let's look at a more sophisticated type. This fellow's a little different. "Good morning, Mr. Manager. I'm not really looking for a job. In fact, I'm one of the most successful guys over where I am, but they don't love me. And I looked at four or five other companies, but I'm not deciding until I know what you have to offer and then I'm going to compare what you have to offer with these others. If you shape up, you might get me." That's like me going to my wife saying, "Honey, I'm looking at five other cuties, but I'm not deciding until I know what you have to offer and if you shape up you might get me." She wouldn't get much, would she? And neither does the company get much who gets a man based on what you're going to give him. The real question is, what are you going to give them?

Listen, a company's got nothing to give. A company is a group of people. If you join a company to get something, all you're going to do is bleed it dry and then you're all going to be miserable. Sometimes a guy says, "Hey, we've got room for you! Six guys just quit!"

When I came into the life insurance business, I'll never forget a guy told me about the life insurance policy. He actually sold me a life insurance policy. I never believed in life insurance. My best friend went into the life insurance business. Naturally, he came to see me first. He told me this story I couldn't get over. Great insurance, waive a premium, cash that boosts your collateral, twice as much back as you put into retirement. I said, "Sign me up!" And then he told me how much money he got paid for doing me this favor. I said, "How long has this been going on? I want in on this!" He said, "You've got to take the aptitude."

The Price of Leadership

"The aptitude," I said. "What's that?" He said you've got to pass it to get in. I said, "I'll take it on one condition." He said, "What's that?" I said, "If I flunk it, I can take it over again." What do I care what the aptitude says? I want in on this!

The manager told me about the freedom, the dough, and the prestige. What do you think was the first thing I discovered after I got in the business? The manager lied! If I would have known how bad he needed me I wouldn't have cheated on that lousy aptitude! Well, anyway, he fooled me and I fooled him and that's where it stopped. I could've traded him in on a new model, but nothing's doing. I made up my mind. I'd die there, and that's always worked out pretty good.

I guess it is silly believing you'll never quit. I recommend everybody quit one time in their life. You see, business is like a marriage. You have courtships. You may have been with companies before the one you're with now, but I want to tell you this. You're never going to be successful, really successful anywhere, unless right where you are now you're married to the job—the company you're with right now. Unless you're married, you cannot be really successful.

Because, you see, the real success in any job is more than just the money you get. You can get money anywhere. You can get a deal anywhere.

Charlie "Tremendous" Jones

You can get many things marriage offers anywhere, but you can't get a marriage. You see, a marriage is something more. Now remember this: you can court companies, but someday you've got to get married and die for the eyes that you committed to. You are the company. Who are you going to live your life with? What are you going to be? And last, what are you to live it for?

Several years ago I was in Palm Springs, California, and a fellow was speaking and closed his talk. There were only thirty-one of us, and thirty-one of these men had done $500 million worth of business collectively the year before. Now this guy didn't need to tell us how to recruit or manage or sell. We knew that better than he did. But I'll tell you one thing this guy did. He was smart. He second-guessed us. He closed his talk and he said, "Men, you're not ready to live your lives until you know what you want written on your tombstone." I thought, *Hmmm, I'll need a big monument!* No, what he meant was what are you going to be alive for? I never thought of it that way before, but did many times after hearing that.

There's only two things to live your life for, only two. The first is for *numero uno*; me, myself, and I. You know, the chest beater, the "Hey, world, look at me, ain't I grand?" You know the guy? The self-made jackass. "I'm a self-made man!" Well, good for you! That relieves God of that responsibility. But don't ever hate those guys too much. Remember, we've all been like this. Nobody's ever gone through life that wasn't like this at some point. Some of you may not be yet, but you will.

But there are two things you can live your life for. You can live it as if the sun rises and sets on you, or you can let God live it for you. That's right. You can live it for you or let God live it for you. You say, "Charlie, are you a theologian?" No. "Are you a Bible teacher?" Not really. "Ever had any Bible training?" No. "Well, why do you say that?" Well, it's just a matter of simple fact that you don't begin to live without finding out the two ways to live life. *You* live it or *God* lives it.

I get asked if I am one of these guys who believe God solves your problems. On the contrary! According to the scriptures, God doesn't solve your problems. He gives you a fresh batch. You see, when you really begin to live—I mean, really live—He isn't calling you to a picnic grounds. He's calling you to triumphant warfare. You see throughout the Bible men engaged in triumphant warfare and not on picnic grounds.

And a guy says, "Charlie, are you one of these

people who believes people should believe what you believe?" No, I never tell people to believe what I believe, nor do I tell them to believe because I believe. But I do tell them this: Know what you're going to live your life in, know who you're going to live it with, and know what you're going to live it for. Know you're living for yourself, or know you're living it for God. But don't straddle the fence.

Now, when I came in the life insurance business, I was against God. And I knew why I was against Him. I had a lot of good reasons to be against Him. I was raised with a bunch of religious hypocrisy. I remember as a boy my dad used to say, "Son, you've got to quit drinking, smoking, swearing, gambling." I said, "Wait a minute, Pop, I might as well go to hell right now. What am I going to do with all my time?" And somebody else will say, "Jones, you've got to learn to hate sin." I'd say, "Hate sin? I love it. I never took a sinner lesson in my life, it just comes natural."

Somebody else will say, you need God and God needs you! I'd say, "God needs me? If God needs me, it's too late for him!" And then some real religious guy would say, "In order to get to heaven you've got to do the best you can." How 'bout that? Why, everybody knows nobody ever did the best they could! Everybody knows that everybody could do a little better. That if they tried a little bit harder and wanted to do a little bit more, they could, couldn't they? So based on what all these religious guys were saying, I knew I was going to hell in style and that everybody else would be surprised to meet me there.

Well, I couldn't hold out with my wife. She nagged me into joining the church. So there I was in my hometown, with hundreds and hundreds of my friends, standing before the pastor, and he asks, "Do you believe this?" Yes. "Do you believe that?" Yes. I lied to everything he asked me. But I knew all my friends lied too, and I thought, *Who am I to upset the apple cart this late in the game?* At the end of the sermon, the pastor gave the right hand of fellowship with one hand and a pack of envelopes in the other, and I was in.

Now, I'm not making fun of the church. I love the church! But I'll tell you what I hate. I hate double-talk. I hate mental gymnastics. I hate word games. I hate the lies that we parrot and recite, that break hearts and dwarf lives. I want people to be honest, and if they can't be honest I want to cut them off, until they think on certain things and learn to be honest. I had never met an honest person.

One day I'm driving down the street looking

for a prospect and a guy jumps in my car. That was a miracle; most people were jumping out of a salesman's car! He was a truck driver but he sure looked healthy. "Ah, Charlie Jones," he said. "How is it with your soul?" I said, "My what?" He said, "Are you born again?" I said, "Here I am!" I didn't know what he was talking about. He said, "Are you going to heaven?" And then I realized he was a religious fanatic.

When religious people used to approach me and say I needed to be happy, I'd say, "Look I'm happier without what you have than you are with it. If you want to work on somebody, why don't you work on some miserable religious people?" That would scare them off. I would tell them that religion and the Bible are for the ignoramuses and the poverty stricken. It's a myth, fable, poetry, history—nobody believes it anymore. So I gave him a couple of my "pew duster-off"ers" that I'd used on religious people, but it didn't work on him. He was different. He didn't tell me what church he belonged to. He didn't tell me to quit anything or buy anything. He didn't say he was better than I was. He just told me that God is God. The Bible is true. That's it: take it or leave it, that's him. You know what? This was the first real, honest person I had ever really met in this regard. But I didn't want to be converted and I realized he wasn't going to buy any life insurance, so I terminated our interview. And I'll never forget as he got out of my car, he said, "Now Charlie, remember this, the Jew and the Catholic and the Protestant disagree in a lot of things, but they all agree the Bible is the word of God."

He continued, "The Bible is sixty-six books written over sixteen hundred years, by more than forty different men that's come down through the ages and formed a continuity that's challenged the minds and blessed the hearts of thousands of millions of people. Now listen, if the Bible is wrong and you're right, I have nothing to lose. But if the Bible is right and you're wrong, you have everything to lose and your life to spend in hell." Well, that was the greatest case I had ever heard. I made up my mind, I'd not eat another meal, I'd not sell another policy, I'd not do anything until I determined in my heart, is the Bible true?

Well, strangely enough, that afternoon I'd read about the autobiographies of men and about the religions of the world. I read everything I could to disprove this nonsense, this idiocy of religion. But for the first time in my life that afternoon I realized, strangely, for some reason or another, that the Bible was true. I made up my mind that if I decided it was true, I'd believe it and accept it. But if it wasn't true, I made up my mind too that I was going to throw it in the trash can, sleep in Sunday morning, and save a dollar a week because I felt the pastor was gypping me anyway.

That afternoon when I bowed my head in my car in Lancaster, Pennsylvania, I just simply said, "God, I want you to forgive me and come into my heart. I don't understand all this business about religion but I know I'm a sinner. I want you to come into my heart and make me whatever a Christian really is. Amen." I thought I would hear bells ring or something. I expected something, and nothing happened. And I thought, *Well, maybe God thought I was praying one of my old-fashioned prayers.* I used to pray often, *Lord, let me get hot tonight.* But I was praying the first sincere prayer of my life. I was praying from the bottom of my heart, just simply saying, *God, I really want to know, I really want to know you.*

I didn't care what it cost, I didn't care. *I'm not looking for an escape. I just want to know you, that's all I really want to know, I just want to know you. Come into my heart and help my unbelief.* That was my prayer. As I bowed my head again, I said, *Lord, I really mean business,* something like that, *Amen.* And I raised my head again. And you know what I didn't get? I never got a feeling.

But you know, I thought I was going to get a feeling when I got married. I knew when I got her, signed, sealed, and delivered, I knew how I would feel. I would feel that married feeling. I stood in front of the pastor and he said, "I now pronounce you man and wife." There I was, a married man, and I didn't feel any different! A couple weeks later, I woke up one night and I said, "Honey, honey, I don't feel married anymore." She said, "You are just the same. Don't you try to get out of it!"

Well, listen, I never got the married feeling when I got married. I never got the *insurancey* feeling when I got into insurance. I never got a religious feeling when I came to know God. Don't you pity people who run their lives by feelings? Life is a great thing when you know who you're going to live it with, what you're going to live it in, what are you going to live it for. That's tremendous, isn't it?

The next price of leadership is *weariness*. WEARINESS. If you are going to do anything worthwhile, you're always going to be surrounded by people who will never be doing their share. There's always going to have to be some people who are willing to do more than their share that take care of all of the people who are not doing their share. That's right. A lot of people think this is the age of relaxation. Slow down; take it easy; pace yourself. Listen! You will never be able to slow down, take it easy, and pace yourself. Remember that verse: to him that much is given, much is expected. That's right. You can call yourself a leader, you can have the title, you can have the position, you can have the endowment, but unless you're paying the price, those things mean nothing.

People used to say to me, "Charlie, Charlie, slow down, you're going to burn yourself out, you're going to die young!" They'd say I ought to get a hobby. I'd say, "I ought to get a hobby? I've got six kids! I've got a wonderful job! What do I need a hobby for?" "Oh, you've got to get a hobby to get away from it all." Get away from it all? I'm trying to get *into* it all!

Although a leader should be on guard for the pitfall of overextension, a leader must also deal with the reality that he or she must often go the extra mile. The leader learns that the sense of responsibility comes only to a few, and if your church, community, or company is to go on, you must carry the load that you and you alone can carry. You can give up when you want, lay it down, but remember: no one can pay your price.

So I went down to buy myself a motorboat. They sold me a cabin cruiser. There I was, Captain Jones! Was I relaxed? No! I was worried to death who was selling my prospects back on dry land! I'm a trustee over here at a fine little college. One night we had a speaker speaking on interdenominational foreign missions. And as I heard this guy speak on the needs of people in other countries and I thought of me riding around on that boat, I couldn't take it. I sold that lousy cabin cruiser and gave every nickel to the missionary fund. Since then, I have been so relaxed I can hardly hold myself together!

So a guy says, "Charlie, are you against hobbies?" I'm not against hobbies, I'm not against anything, but I'm for some things. One of the things I'm for is earning the right to enjoy some things. I'm sick and tired of people spending money they don't have to buy things they don't need to impress people they don't like! I earned twenty-five thousand dollars a year before I earned a wrist watch. I broke it three weeks ago in Tampa. I was just learning that it's better to want things you don't have than have things you don't want.

Leaders must be growing. We are aware that growth requires growing pains, and that growth so often comes through failure. A young fellow asked an old-timer how he became successful. The old-timer replied, "Good judgment." The young fellow then asked, "How did you get that?" The old-timer replied, "Experience." The young fellow asked again, "How did you get *that*?" And the old-timer replied, "Poor judgment!"

Another wearisome phrase leaders often hear is, "It isn't worth it." There are going to be times when a leader will make tremendous sacrifices only to feel that it isn't worth it. Leaders are learning that they live lives not of choice, but of necessity. They find that they must do what has to be done, not what they want to do. Leaders find it wearisome, trying to do the impossible.

I'll tell you what makes it worse. Do you know one of the main ways a person really grows? It is by failure. It's a sure thing that's the way you grow. That way there is wisdom with being any kind of a leader. If you're going to lead, you're going to know what it is to fail.

I'll tell you another thing that makes it worse than being a leader. Every person is born with a thin skin and hard heart. It's worse going through that process of transforming a thin skin and hard heart to a thick skin and a soft heart, isn't it?

You heard about the guy who went in to see the prospect and the prospect insulted him. That wasn't covered in the basic course, so he went back to the office to see the manager but the manager was out taking his afternoon nap. And he said to the old-timer, "What do you do if you get insulted?" The old-timer says, "I don't know." The guy says, "How long have you been here?" The old-timer says, "Twenty-five years." The guy says, "Twenty-five years? You've never been insulted?" The old-timer says, "Let's see, I been kicked, beat up, spit on, and thrown out, but no one ever insulted me." You know what? The average guy, if you blow on him the wrong way, he blows away. You know why? He still has that lousy thin skin and hard heart. How'd you like to belong to an agency where everybody had a thin skin and hard heart? Well, you can't change the agency, but you can change you and it's a wearisome process. It's a wearisome process of going through what it takes to get a thick skin and a soft heart.

It's like the guy who went in to see his first prospect of the day. He said, "Good morning, sir, I'd like to tell you about my idea." The prospect said, "I wish you'd shut your big fat mouth. Who let you in here? Get off my property! If I catch you in here again, I'll have you arrested!" The salesman smiled and said, "I wish I had a hundred prospects like you." The prospect said, "Why?" He said, "Because I've got a thousand like you!"

You know another thing that makes it worse being a leader? Another thing that makes it worse being a leader is those people always over in the corner howling, "It isn't worth it, it isn't worth

Charlie "Tremendous" Jones

it, it isn't worth it!" Well, who in the world said it was? Let me tell you, I don't know of one guy doing a job that doesn't know cost. No money could pay him to do what he's doing if he's doing a real job. No money. You know why he's doing it? I'll tell you why he's doing it. He's doing it because somebody has to do it, and if somebody doesn't do the things that have to be done around where he's working, then where he's working won't be worth being a part of, now, will it?

If anybody ever asks you if it's worth it, don't answer them because they wouldn't understand the right answer if you gave it to them. And if they would understand, they wouldn't have asked the silly question in the first place, would they? No. That's what my wife used to ask me, and I never answered her. But I don't ask her, "Is it worth it?" Some of the things she has to do I know aren't worth it. She does it because she has to do it.

And let's not forget about the critics! How come everybody who's not doing anything always knows how to do what you're trying to do better than you're trying to do it? Don't they drive you nuts? If I were the leader I'd have to be like the Indian chief who was drafted into the army. The first day he was there they blew the bugle and woke him up. They blew the bugle to put the flag up. They blew the bugle to come in and eat breakfast. They blew the bugle to eat lunch. They blew the bugle to eat supper. They blew the bugle to put him to sleep. Every time the poor Indian turned around, they blew the bugle. They had him sleeping with the generals, the colonels, the captain, the lieutenant, the corporal. And after a few days of this, he walks in and he says, "Me quit on the army." The captain says, "You can't quit on the army." He says, "Me no like in the army." The captain says, "What don't you like about it?" He says, "Too much toot 'em and salute 'em and not enough shoot 'em!"

You know the difference between a leader and nonleader? I was at Palm Springs yesterday, and a really sharp, sophisticated guy from New York City says, "I don't go to any meetings! I don't go for that!" I chewed him up and spit him out. He doesn't go to meetings and he wanted somebody to give him a good reason to go to meetings. He didn't realize that leaders all go to meetings. They go to meetings to give because that's the only way you ever get anything out of a meeting! It's always good to hear what somebody says. They go to listen to somebody bounce some things off of them, which provokes them to think so they can get to the firing line and make something happen. That's the difference between a leader who comes to a meeting and goes out and makes something happen and somebody else who comes in and sits around and goes out and sits around.

A guy rushed in to see the doctor and says, "Doctor, doctor, I've got troubles!" The doc says, "What's wrong?" He says, "Well, Doc, I sleep alright at night, I sleep alright in the morning, but I toss and turn all afternoon!" Listen, there are a lot of people who are weary for the wrong reasons!

The next price of leadership is *abandonment*. ABANDONMENT. There's not enough time for me to do what I like to do and want to do and need to do and ought to do. We had an all-day workshop. I just love to spend the time on the thought processes. It's hard to take three hours out sometimes, but you know the biggest battles are all fought in our minds. We've got to be learning to abandon what we like to think about and what we want to think about, in favor of what we need to think about and ought to think about. You know the biggest battles you'll ever fight, and do you know what? You'll never lick the battle until it gets worse and worse and worse and worse. A lot of people say they're not fighting a battle. They're right, if you're not in it, you'll never know what it is to have any victories. You'll sit on the sideline and cough and sputter, never blast off the launching pad. You'll never know what it is to lead. But if you really entered into the life of reality, you know what it is to fight battles and you know the battles get worse.

There just isn't time to do all you want to do and all that you should do. It is easy for us to teach abandonment to others, but leaders know the price of abandonment, beginning with their own thought processes. What do you think about? Let's go a step further: what do you *talk* about? Someone once said that little people talk about things, medium-sized people talk about people, and big people talk about ideas. Which kind of people do you like to be around? How are your reading habits? How many books have you read this year? How many are you reading now? How many of the ideas you've received from the books have you shared? The power of a single book at the right time in a person's life is unlimited. The leader leads the way, showing that leaders are readers. You should not only keep a flow of books running through your hands, but give them away to others, too. Paperbacks are inexpensive and popular. I even prepared a book list that points out the books that have been most influential in my life. It was Mac McMillon whom I first heard say, "You are today what you'll be five years from now, except for the books you read and the people you meet."

Learning to think what you ought to think

about, need to think about, like to think about, and want to think about . . . then what do you talk about? Do you talk about what you like to talk about and want to talk about? Do you talk about what you need to talk about? Well, we're just going to take a minute and talk about what you do with your time. Do you do what you like to do and want to do or need to do and ought to do? And there's a difference between what you want and need. You never learned it too well, but you'd better be working at it because your kids won't buy it unless they see it in action.

I used to say, "Well, I never was much of a reader." Oh, you don't have to be much of a reader. I never was much of a reader. Several years ago, I got a hold of Dorothea Brande's book, *Wake Up and Live!* What a book. Dorothea asks, "Do you want to be a success?" Yes! "You really do?" Yes! "Are you sure you do?" Yes! She says, "Then how come you try so hard to be a failure?" Since I read her book, I never told anybody I want to be a success anymore, because she proved to me that I still do more every day to be a failure than I do to be a success. A guy says, "Well, wait a minute, if you do more every day to be a failure than you do to be a success, how come you're so successful?" I say, "Can I help it if everybody's trying to fail harder than I am?"

The Price of Leadership

You've got to know the problem before you can do anything about it. What does it take to be a success? Courage, confidence, love, joy, peace, meekness, faith, humility. You name it, I hardly have any of those qualities. What does it take to be a failure? Thanklessness, cowardice, procrastination, cynicism, callousness. You name it, I'm loaded with those!

Of course, some people never recognize what the Bible's all about, so they never get into it. As I read *Wake Up and Live!* my thinking changed. She pointed out how we all have a built-in rule to fail. Some of us fail and act like we're successful at it. Many even enjoy failure and try to justify it. At first they cover it up, but nobody really ever gets up and says, *Whew, I'm a self-made failure!* But that's what they are.

Somebody gave me a copy of *Think and Grow Rich*. What a book! I wish somebody would've given me that earlier. I was rereading it the second time flying down to Alabama for a convention a couple years ago. As I read that second chapter, I had to turn my face over to the window of the plane because I didn't want the stewardess to see me crying. You say, "You were crying reading *Think and Grow Rich*?" Yes, I was reading the part about the father with the deaf and dumb boy. He loved that boy so much and was so dedicated. He was such a positive thinker. He sold that kid on what a blessing it was to be deaf and dumb, and he sold the kid on going through public school. What a privilege it was to go to a public school! The kid grew up realizing that he was a special, privileged character. Because he was deaf and dumb, he got special treatment in school. The kids who weren't deaf and dumb didn't get the good treatment he got. He went on through college and grew up to become a great, positive, contributing factor in his community. As I read about that kind of dedication of that dad, my heart broke and I said, "Oh God, I pray that someday I'll have that kind of dedication for my six kids. I don't have it now, but God, by your grace, I sure hope I can have it someday."

When I began to read this book, my own heart began to change and my life began to be seasoned and things began to be different. I firmly believed that you only get to enjoy what you give away, so I used to buy one hundred copies of this book and five hundred copies of this book. Everybody who came through my office would get a book. The National Test Register man would get a book, the IBM man would get a book, everybody would get a book. If you didn't want a book, you'd get a book anyway. Everybody gets a book. You say, "Well, what if he didn't want to read?" Listen, you can take a horse to water but you can't make him drink. That's true, but you can put salt in his oats and make him thirsty! I was just salting his oats. He'd come around eventually.

It's funny how we always miss the boat at the most important place. Why is it we always come to the right place last? Why is it? I used to be awful critical of them in Washington until one day I learned I was running a worse program at my home than the president was down there!

A guy says, "Wait a minute, Charlie! Aren't you ever discouraged?" Yes I am. But if I get discouraged, I'll never let you know about it. Because if I get discouraged and let you know about it, you'll get discouraged. And if you get discouraged you'll discourage me back, and I can hardly stand how much I already have. My wife taught me that. I used to go home and she'd say, "How'd it go, dear?" I'd say, "Don't you ask me how it goes. Here I am starving, working my finger to the bone, and the lousy home office just started another contest on urine specimens and I'm sick of the whole load." I'd say, "How'd it go with you?" She'd say, "It's a good thing you got home. Those kids are driving me nuts and the washer broke!" And then she'd get unhappier and I'd get unhappier, and pretty soon there was trouble.

Now I go home and I've learned that the roof

Charlie "Tremendous" Jones

has caved in, the walls have fallen down, the men have quit, and the business is lost. The sheriff is closing in. I walk in and my wife says, "How'd it go today, dear?" I say, "Whew, I sure hope things don't get any better! I'm so tired of being happy, it's wearing me out! How'd it go with you?" She says, "Pretty good." As she gets happier, I get happier. I get happier, she gets happier. Now we're so happy we can't stand it anymore! You may think we're nuts, but you're nuts. But look how much fun it is!

I made a rule years ago that I'll die before I ever let anybody know I'm discouraged. That's right. A guy says, "Wait a minute, wait a minute! Don't you think you're a hypocrite for acting happy when you're miserable?" I say, "Don't you think you're a hypocrite for acting miserable when you were happy?" You've got to make up your mind. Do you want to be a happy hypocrite or a miserable hypocrite? I made up my mind: I'm a happy hypocrite! I'm gettin' rich. Woo-hoo!

I have a little three-year-old, Tracey. I'll see Tracey tomorrow night, and when I see Tracey, I'll say, "Hi Tracey, how are you?" She'll say, "Tremendous!" I'll say, "How are things going?" She'll say, "I hope things don't get any better." I'll say, "Why?" She says, "Because I'm so tired of being happy it's wearing me out!"

The Price of Leadership

I believe it's the greatest sin for a man to go into his office or his home discouraged. I believe it's the greater sin for a man to go into his office or his home discouraged than it is to go down the aisle of his church drunk. That's right. I believe more harm is done by discouragement than liquor. And I believe, as the Apostle Paul said, he'd give up eating meat to keep from offending his brethren. I believe the least I can do is give up being discouraged so I don't offend any of my friends.

A leader does not let his circumstances dictate his attitude. But a leader learns to have an attitude of gratitude even in the midst of negative or discouraging circumstances. Paul Speicher once said it another way: "An attitude of gratitude flavors everything you do." Thankfulness is the sign of the big person; thanklessness is the sign of the little person. Are you the most thankful person you've ever met? If not, *why* not? Remember, you'll never be thankful for everything until you learn to be generally thankful for nothing. To learn to be thankful for the privilege of *being* thankful is one of the marks of greatness.

The fourth and final price of leadership is *vision*. VISION. We cannot pay the price of leadership without knowing where we are going and what we are doing. How easy it is to lay out what we want, but how difficult it is to find the real pathway to it. Perspective is vital. The scriptures have expressed it perfectly: "Where there is no vision, the people perish." Certainly, this is multiplied for the leader. I think that if I could have one wish granted, I'd ask that I be permitted to see clearly, ten minutes a day. If that could be done, the world would beat a path to my door because even the saints have had to look through a glass darkly.

One of the most exciting thoughts that ever came into my mind was the discovery of what vision really is. I had thought perhaps it was unusual imagination or creativity. No—as in all things, the *best* things are all at our feet, free and ready to be put to use. Vision is *being able to see things as they are.* I think much is gained by studying those whose lives have stood the test of time, those who saw things as they really were.

Lincoln was a man of vision. One of his many great quotations hangs in my office: "I have been driven many times to my knees by the overwhelming conviction that I had nowhere else to go—my own wisdom and that of all about me seemed insufficient for that day." Lincoln has taught me that no one ever truly grows up until he learns to go down.

Daniel Webster was a man of vision. He was

The Price of Leadership

asked once what he considered the most important thought that ever entered his mind, to which he replied, "My personal accountability to Almighty God." Webster knew that everyone, some day, stands for judgment, to give an account, and his account was in the hands of a Lawyer who has never lost a case.

Patrick Henry was a man of vision. His spine-tingling speech, "Give me liberty or give me death," attests to this. The reason Patrick Henry could shout this with conviction is revealed in his last will and testament, where he writes, "My most cherished possession, I wish I could leave you, my Faith in Jesus Christ, for with him and nothing else, you can be happy, but without Him and nothing else, you'll never be happy."

Roger Hull closed an address with, "A man can be born with ability, he can acquire knowledge, he can develop skill, but wisdom comes only from God." We all need wisdom to be parents, citizens, employers, and employees. There is no place to buy wisdom, no secular university that teaches it. No one can lead who doesn't know how to follow or who to follow. Where will we get our wisdom? Who are we following? How is our vision?

We began with a story to illustrate my attitude in approaching this subject. I'd like to close with a similar story that will sum up all I've tried to say.

Charlie "Tremendous" Jones

Once there was a boy rowing an old-timer across a wide river. As they rowed on, the old-timer picked a leaf from the water. He studied it for a while and then asked the boy, "Son, do you know anything about biology?" The boy replied, "No sir, I don't." The old-timer said, "Son, you have missed 25 percent of your life." As they rowed on, the old-timer took a rock from the bottom of the boat, and as he held it in his hand studying, he asked the boy, "Son, do you know anything about geology?" The boy sheepishly replied, "No sir, I don't." The old-timer said, "Son, you've missed 50 percent of your life." As they rowed on, the twilight came and the old-timer began to study the North Star that had begun to twinkle. After a while, he asked the boy, "Son, do you know anything about astronomy?" The boy, with head low and embarrassed, replied, "No sir, I don't." The old-timer quickly and forcefully said, "Son, you've missed 75 percent of your life." Just then, out of the corner of his eye, the boy noticed the huge dam upstream beginning to crumble and the water pouring over in torrents. Quickly he turned to the old-timer and shouted, "Sir, do you know how to swim?" The old-timer replied, "No, I don't." The boy shouted back, "YOU JUST LOST YOUR LIFE!"

We may not know all the methods and techniques, we may not be the greatest recruiters or motivators, but we have to be real students of living if we are to pay the price of leadership, for the price of leadership is really nothing more than *really living.*

The *Life-Changing Classics* and *Laws of Leadership* series bring you timeless wisdom in compact, affordable editions! Available now at www.TremendousLifeBooks.com!

Share the warmth, wisdom and humor of beloved speaker and author Charlie "Tremendous" Jones!

- Books
- CDs
- DVDs

...And much more at Charlie's home on the web, www.TremenodusLifeBooks.com